# What Thought Leaders Are about the Perfect Day Method

*"Pierre Khawand demonstrates how simple visuals can not only help you navigate a "perfect day" but also help him explain the concepts behind working in short, productive bursts of attention. His visual depiction of the "Results Curve" is, literally, eye opening. I love his argument for using paper journals to anchor your progress."*

-- David Sibbet, Bestselling Author, President and Founder, The Grove Consultants International

*"The PDM approach helps me create a consistent structure and process for a multi-tasking, multi-lingual and multi-project work environment that often defies time zones. It is an easy method to integrate with my tools as I always carry a notebook for my ideas and thoughts throughout the day."*

-- Karina Jensen, Practice Director, Centre for Leadership and Effective Organizations, Professor, Global Innovation and Leadership, NEOMA Business School, France

*"In a world saturated with inputs and information, we need something to clear the clutter and focus on what truly matters. Pierre's time-tested tactics will help you do just that, in short powerful bursts that add up to significant accomplishments. Read this book, practice the principles, and watch your work transform 15 minutes at a time."*

-- Jenny Blake, author of Pivot: The Only Move That Matters is Your Next One

*"Behind every successful strategic plan is an intense focus on execution. The Perfect 15-Minute Day Method enables teams to reach their strategic goals 15 minutes at a time, providing individuals and organizations a competitive advantage in today's information deluge. In addition to step-by-step instructions, the book demonstrates how key elements of the method are supported by neuroscientific research. A must read for today's executives and their teams to avoid scattered minds and execute to achieve their strategic goals."*

-- Adrian C. Ott, Award-Winning Author, The 24-Hour Customer, CEO Exponential Edge Inc.

"As a psychiatrist who specializes in treating ADHD, I know the importance of structure and the value of tools that can be used to create this structure. This book provides an excellent tool to structure one's time. Unlike most books tackling time management issues, this book goes a step farther by addressing not just the mental, but also emotional factors affecting productivity.

"My ADHD patients often experience overwhelm with their to-do lists. This method gives a much needed structure to accomplish these tasks, in a manageable way."

-- Alicia R. Maher, M.D., Board Certified Psychiatrist, Subspecialty Board Certified, Psychosomatic Medicine, Akasha Center for Integrative Medicine, Santa Monica, CA, UCLA School of Medicine Clinical Faculty

# What Users Are Saying about the Perfect Day Method

*"[I] can finally remember what it is like to love my job again!"*
--Rachel Ungar

*"I became more mindful of what I was doing throughout the day without being a slave to the clock."* -- Julie Meyer

*"I became more aware of how I get distracted and learned some ways to limit the distractions and to resist the pull of e-mail."* --Ann T.

*"Big insights [from the method] were the value of making your to- do list and actions visible and becoming more aware of how much time things take to do."* --Susan Templeton

*"[The method] helped me prioritize and focus on the things I really wanted to get done."* -- Audrey Plough

*"[The method] provided me with great clarity on how I'm spending my time during the day and where I trip myself up.* -- Amy Koh

*"It is simple and direct enough to be useful all the time."* -- Rosanne Belpedio

*"[One of the top three benefits of the method is] getting things done that I may have been procrastinating on."* -- Jeff Fanselow

*"[I gained] a sense of calm and control."* --Katie Uckele

*"Total success"* -- Tiffany Conn

# the PERFECT 15-MINUTE DAY

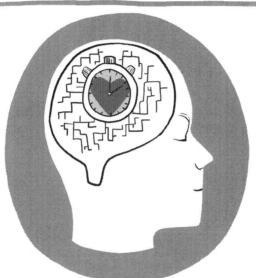

Managing your
TIME · THOUGHTS · EMOTIONS

Pierre Khawand

© 2016 OnTheGo Technologies, LLC. All rights reserved.

ISBN-13: 978-1532783814

ISBN-10: 1532783817

# About Pierre Khawand

Pierre Khawand has more than twenty years of experience in the software industry. He has led several technology ventures, completed successful mergers and acquisitions, and founded People-OnTheGo in 2001. His Accomplishing More Leadership Program helps today's leaders develop the awareness and behaviors needed to focus on results and develop people in the midst of the information overload. His bestselling Accomplishing More With Less workshop is enabling today's business professionals make breakthroughs in their work and personal lives. Pierre holds a Master's degree in Engineering from the University of Michigan, and has completed several Executive Education programs at the Stanford Graduate School of Business (Stanford California). When not tackling productivity issues, Pierre enjoys hikes with his wife and friends in the San Francisco area, as well as Tai Chi and Argentine Tango.

# Also by Pierre Khawand

- *Time for Leadership*
- *The Results Curve*
- *The Accomplishing More With Less Workbook*
- *Accomplishing More With Google Apps*
- *The New New Inbox*
- *The Perfect 15-Minute Day Journal*

# Acknowledgements

First, I would like to thank the early adopters of the Perfect 15-Mintue Day Method who contributed tremendously to the refinement of the method and who helped us confirm that there is hope for managing the overload, feeling calmer and happier in the workplace and beyond.

Special thanks to the People-OnTheGo team, especially Sarah Tang for her dedicated effort in research and writing, and her valuable insights throughout this journey, and Katie Uckele for her extensive research that helped support the method every step of the way, and Claire Donaldson for helping make the book visual and user friendly.

Last but not least, thanks to my family and friends, whose support and engagement have been most instrumental to the completion of this yet another exciting journey.

I hope you enjoy reading *The Perfect 15-Minute Day* and take these habits to your work and personal life to create accomplishments and happiness for you, your team, your organization, and your community!

# Table of Contents

# Chapter 1

# Getting started

We live in a world of overload, no doubt about it!

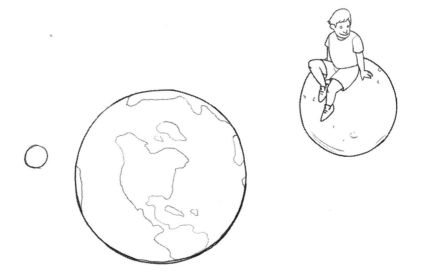

Unless you have been on some other planet for some time, you already
know and feel the overload in some way or another: too many e-mails, too

much social media, too many competing and changing priorities, too many interruptions. Worse, we are led to believe that we need to keep up, to speed up in order to succeed in the modern workplace.[1] As a result, our minds are overwhelmed and scattered. Studies show that work in an interruptive environment, whether or not those interruptions are related to our work, increases the experience of stress, frustration, time pressure, and effort to get the work done.[2]

---

[1] "Time and Time Again: The Search for Meaning/fulness Through Popular Discourse on the Time and Timing of Work" by Dawna I. Ballard and Sunshine P. Webster

[2] "The Cost of Interrupted Work: More Speed and Stress" by Gloria Mark, Daniela Gudith, and Ulrich Klocke (2008)

# The Perfect 15-Minute Day Method (PDM) comes to the rescue

After the success of the Accomplishing More in Less Time, With Less Effort, and Less Stress methodology [3], with thousands of business professionals achieving significant breakthroughs as a result, we

---

[3] The Accomplishing More With Less Workbook, The Accomplishing More With Less Workshop, The Accomplishing More Leadership Program.

continued to explore new ways to overcome the overload and help business professionals regain their ability to focus so as to feel happier and more fulfilled at work. Thus, PDM was born.

# At the end of the day, a happier you!

Participants who tested and helped refine PDM were fascinated by how simple and how powerful it is, that is, simple in its application but powerful in its outcome. They reported feeling significantly less scattered and better able to manage interruptions, stay focused, and quickly recover from inevitable interruptions; they also felt better at estimating how long tasks would take, and utilizing their time more strategically. Participants also reported that they felt less stressed, that they stopped more often to acknowledge their accomplishments, and felt fulfilled and motivated. They were happy!

# All you need is a journal and a timer

With just a journal and a timer, PDM helps you a) *be always aware of what you're working on* and b) *stay focused on the task at hand by working in highly productive bursts of short 15-minute increments.* The method includes the use of tags to help you track your tasks, manage interruptions, manage thoughts and emotions along the way, and be able to reconcile and close the loops on unfinished items at the end of the day.

Studies confirm that we work in a highly interruptive work environment, and find that most of us use tools like post-its, planners, and e-mail printouts to help us maintain our attention and keep track of information from all our different tasks.[4] The journal exceeds this function. While post-its, planners, and e-mail printouts remind us of important tasks, they often are not organized by priority - or organized at all. Too often these items are scattered in the workspace and easy to lose track of. The PDM journal is organized to simply and efficiently inform us of tasks and their priority. It also unifies your notes and provides a great audit trail.

---

[4] "Constant, Constant, Multi-tasking Craziness: Managing Multiple Working Spheres" (2004) by Victor M. González and Gloria Mark

If you're thinking "but I do everything electronically", you will soon discover the journal perfectly supplements the electronic world and plays an important role in helping us gain depth and perspective.

While many of the PDM techniques can be done digitally to the same success, the PDM journal has a key advantage over digital task management assistants - it is always visible and can be constantly consulted. The journal will not be minimized while you are tasking. Taking notes in the journal is less intrusive, usually much quieter, and much faster than opening a note-taking app. Often we get distracted in the process of accessing a digital note-taking app. The journal is simple enough to quickly capture an item without distracting you. Plus, a journal can be with you at all times. It takes no time to get it out and open it, and it never runs out of battery.

We suggest trying a paper journal first, then, if you feel you can effectively integrate the method digitally, feel free to do so.

# Why 15 minutes, you ask?

    Anything shorter is not long enough to make meaningful progress on most work-related tasks, and anything longer loses its immediacy and risks our getting lost in time. The 15-minute increment is both short enough to keep us focused and long enough for us to accomplish something.

Your timer should always be set to 15 minutes, and reset to 15 minutes. Having a defined allotment of time frees you of making a decision every time you take on a task. Making a decision takes time and energy that could be better spent working on your task.

Note that the 15 minutes is not a deadline. It is an intention and a checkpoint. It means: "I intend to focus on this task for up to 15 minutes and then check to see if I am on the right track or if I want to adjust." It is about becoming aware of time instead of getting lost in time.

The 15-minute mark doesn't limit you from working more on a task. Once the timer beeps you can renew your intention to work on that task for another 15 minutes, and yet another one, and therefore work on the task for a cumulative 45 minutes, or longer. The idea is that you have checkpoints so you can be more conscious of the time decisions that you are making.

While it may be tempting to choose a time increment other than 15 minutes, we urge you to start with the 15-minute increment and stick to it for a week at first. In fact, studies show that people already work in fragmented amounts of time averaging about 12 minutes of continuous work on a task before switching to another.[5] Thus 15 minutes of focus is more than enough to ask for in today's busy workday. Most users discover that the 15-minute time increment is just right and continue to use it. Some tailor it to 20 or 30 minutes.

---

[5] "Constant, Constant, Multi-tasking Craziness: Managing Multiple Working Spheres" (2004) by Victor M. González and Gloria Mark

# PDM helps you manage your thoughts and your emotions

After all, and before all, we are humans! We have thoughts and emotions of all kinds, some more productive than others. How we handle these thoughts and emotions, especially the unproductive ones, can have a profound impact on our stress level, our mood, our accomplishments, our relationships, and our happiness. Unless we are equipped with the tools we need to become aware of these thoughts and emotions and effectively manage them, we are bound to a less satisfying or even persistently frustrating existence. PDM provides you with the tools and techniques that are needed to manage thoughts and emotions.

# PDM turns you into a multi-tasking guru

True multi-tasking--which consists of performing multiple tasks exactly at the same time like computers with multiple processors, is not possible for us humans. Instead, we switch between the tasks at hand, thinking that we are multi-tasking.

This form of multi-tasking (or task switching) is inefficient and tiring, largely because of the limitations of our short-term memory and inability to keep all the needed information handy as we switch from task to task. The PDM journal solves this issue by allowing us to create the necessary "information stores" to help us switch between, and skillfully handle, the most demanding tasks with ease.

Multi-tasking also contributes to stress and overwork. Studies show that those who multi-task feel like time moves more quickly and that their workload is much heavier than those who focus on a single task.[6] Ideally we would work on a single task on our own pace, but we know this

---

[6] "Simultaneity, Sequentiality, and Speed: Organizational Messages About Multiple-Task Completion" by Keri K. Stephens, Jaehee K. Cho, & Dawna I. Ballard

is not possible in the average workday. Instead, PDM gives us the tools to switch between tasks yet maintain a singular focus.

# PDM helps you achieve mindfulness @work

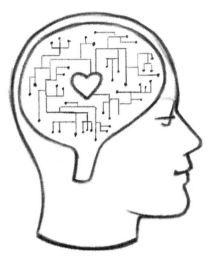

There is growing scientific evidence that mindfulness and mindfulness practices have concrete physical and mental health benefits. MRI scans of meditators compared to non-meditators have shown that mindfulness practices correlate with a thicker cortex in regions of the brain associated with attention and sensory processing.[7] Other research shows that mindfulness practices increase activity in areas of the brain associated with positive emotion, and even boosts the immune system.[8]

The Perfect Day Method is designed to give you the skills to hone your attention and regain control of your time. PDM practices bring mindfulness to your work in a transparent and profound way so you can reap these benefits and experience amazing results. You will discover more about this topic in the Mindfulness @Work chapter.

---

[7] Lazar, S. W., Kerr, C. E., Wasserman, R. H., Gray, J. R., Greve, D. N., Treadway, M. T., ... Fischl, B. (2005). Meditation experience is associated with increased cortical thickness. *Neuroreport, 16*(17), 1893–1897.

[8] Richard Davidson, et al., "Alterations in Brain and Immune Function Produced by Mindfulness Meditation," *Psychosomatic Medicine* 65, no. 4 (2003): 564-570

# PDM is not just a timer technique

Behind the simplicity of PDM lies enormous depth. Don't mistake PDM for a timer technique. While PDM incorporates the timer, similar to some of the popular methods like the Pomodoro Technique and others, PDM is a complete method for managing your time, your thoughts and emotions, your interruptions, and, equally important, for bringing mindfulness and play to your daily work, helping you accomplish amazing things and be happier doing so.

PDM, mostly by design and partly by discovery, leverages science and neuroscience, primary and secondary research, including the feedback from users who have reported major improvements in their work and personal lives as a result.

# In the upcoming chapters

The Results Curve™ chapter provides some of the fundamentals related to how we work and how we achieve results, or not, depending on interruptions and distractions. The chapters that follow explain the method and the insights behind the method. Each chapter begins with a "How it Works" section that explains certain tags or features, and then a "Deeper Meaning" section that explains some of the underlying insights and observations, and finally a "Discoveries" section that portrays some of the observations from users of the method.

# Remember: Your life is a reflection of the next 15 minutes

If you don't know how to manage the next 15 minutes, you don't know how to manage your life. So let us get started!

# Chapter 2

# The Results Curve™

# The Accomplishment Zone™

Let us start by examining how our results change with time when we are working on a task. When we start to work on a task, we start to produce results, and then as we continue to work on that task, we produce more results. This continues until eventually the flow of results begins to level off and then starts to diminish. Results diminish because we get tired, or because we have done what we could and now need to wait for someone else to do their part, or because we have completed the task:

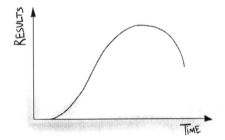

Now let's get back to *real* life. What happens in the real world after we spend a few minutes on a task?

We get interrupted!

E-mail arrives in our inbox and we feel this irresistible urge to check it out, or an instant message (IM) pops up with a compelling proposition. Then there's the phone ringing or a chatty colleague or eager boss stopping by. When an interruption takes place, it prematurely ends the progress on the task at hand:

Post-interruption, when we resume our work on this task, our mind needs to re-retrieve the relevant pieces of information that were let go of during the interruption, and reconstruct the logic and relationships that were previously established. Worse, most people resume a task after dealing with more than two other unrelated tasks; thus re-starting requires more cognitive effort to reorient, and often results in redundant work.[9] This means we will suffer a setback at the restarting point:

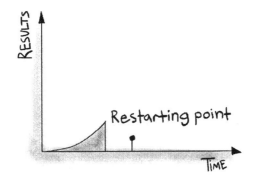

Then we start making progress again, but a few minutes later, another interruption pulls us off task, and our results suffer again. This pattern repeats itself time after time as the calls, emails, and IM's continue.

---

[9] Gloria Mark, Victor M. Gonzalez, and Justin Harris "No Task Left Behind? Examining the Nature of Fragmented Work" (2005)

Interruptions are no longer the exceptions in the digital age – they are the norm. This is our life: a life of interruptions:

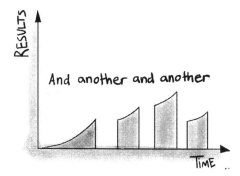

If we compare the actual results that we are getting, represented by the shaded areas below, to the potential results that we could realize if we could manage to stay focused on our task, represented by the Results Curve™, the outcome is nothing less than shocking. We are probably getting a small fraction of the potential results that we would be getting if we were to stay focused:

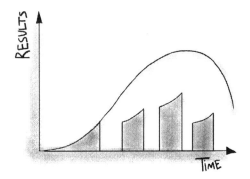

To remedy the situation, you need to stay focused on your task long enough to achieve the desired results. This can take fifteen minutes, thirty minutes, or longer, depending on the task:

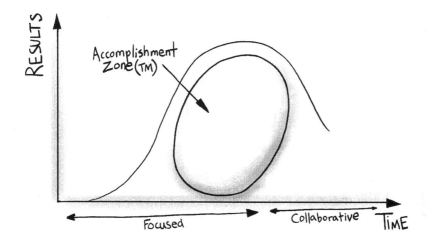

# The Collaborative Zone™

Once you finish the focused session and have accomplished meaningful results, now is the time to stop focusing and switch to being collaborative. This means live interactions with our stakeholders as well as handing e-mail and the like. Just like the focused session, This collaborative session is of paramount importance and likely to bring significant results:

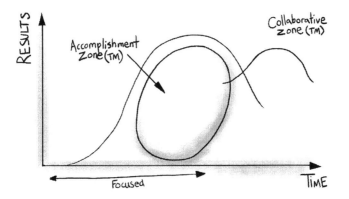

# The Play Zone™

Once you finish the collaborative session, it is time to stop and take a break. This break is intended to help you get refreshed and energized and ready for whatever happens next. We call this break the Play Zone™. It can be short and sweet such as a breathing exercise, stretching for a few minutes, listening to your favorite music, or it can be more involved such as taking a walk around the block:

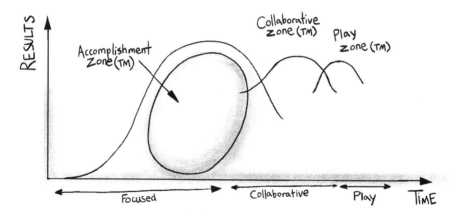

# Three important takeaways from the Results Curve™

- Focus is crucial
- Stopping is essential
- Working in bursts is the name of the game

Focus is critical. As illustrated in the Results Curve™ above, without the focused session, we are *doomed*. We work a few minutes here and a few minutes there, stay at the superficial level, do the quick fixes, and not get deep into our work. We miss the creative and strategic thinking that brings about meaningful accomplishments. As we navigate quickly from one interruption to the next, our brain gets scattered, we get agitated, and soon stressed and overwhelmed.

Stopping is essential. There are three important stops that the Results Curve™ highlights. First is stopping and focusing. Second is stopping the focused effort to collaborate. After all, without collaboration, we can be left in the dark, missing important information, ideas, and contributions from our stakeholders. Third is stopping and getting energized, without which, we can be getting unproductive, ineffective, stressed, and slowly but surely heading to burnout.

Working in bursts is key. This means alternating between focus, collaboration, and play bursts. The length and order of these bursts is all up to you. These depend on the nature of your work and your preferences. Working in bursts is more than just alternating however. It is becoming aware of which phase you are in at any particular time, and purposefully choosing to switch at the right time.

# The Results Curve™ and The Perfect Day Method

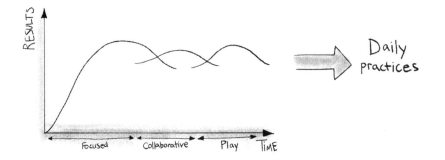

The Perfect Day Method enables you to turn the insights from the Results Curve™ into practical and sustainable behaviors and habits and therefore taking your accomplishments and your happiness to a whole new level. Let's get going!

# Chapter 3

# The Perfect Day

# How it Works

Let's begin by opening your journal. In your journal for each day you will have three pages - a TODAY page, a CAPTURE page, and a NOW page.

## The Today Page

Open your journal to a blank page, title the page TODAY and write down today's date. Below, write a brief outline of what you intend to accomplish today. You may return to this page throughout the day for reference and to add items to the list. That said, you do not need to make an exhaustive or extremely detailed task list. This is intended to be a short list of important items that if accomplished, would make you feel good and bring you closer to accomplishing your bigger goals.

Today's date

What I intend to accomplish today
- Complete the proposal
- Get buy-in on training program
- Identify resources needed to launch loyalty program

# Capture Page

The next page in your journal is your CAPTURE page. Use this page to jot down those to-do items, ideas, and thoughts that pop up throughout the day that you cannot handle immediately, but want to capture and handle at a more convenient time.

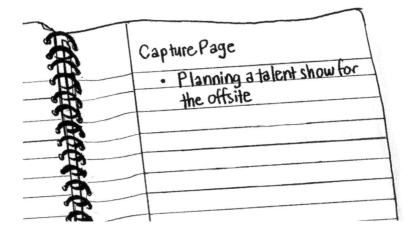

# Now Page

The next page of the journal will be your NOW page. Here you track what you are currently working on, the next steps, and related notes. This page will follow you throughout your day and become a chronological record of your doings. As you will see in the remainder of the book, the NOW page and its tags will help you become more aware of a) how you spend your time, and b) your thoughts and your emotions among other things, and therefore enable you to make better decisions and create a new and improved reality.

The NOW page is organized with tags. For instance, when you start to work on a task, you make a note of it in the NOW page using the NOW: tag. If you are off on a meeting or break, this can be marked with an OFF: tag. The NOW page is not just for NOW: and OFF: tags, but also for MicroPlans™, meeting notes, action items - everything happening right now as you will see soon.

# NOW: and OFF: Tags

As soon as you start to work on a task write

NOW: [the task name] (15)

This means you will work on this task for the next fifteen minutes. Now you know exactly what you're working on, and you set an intention to focus only on this one task for the next fifteen minutes. You solidify this intention by setting the timer and starting. Go!

If you finish your NOW task within the 15-minute timeframe, check it off and move to a new task by making a note of the new task on the NOW page and restarting your timer.

If, however, the timer beeps before you finish your task, you have three choices. You can:

A. Continue
B. Switch to another task
C. Switch to a non-task related activity

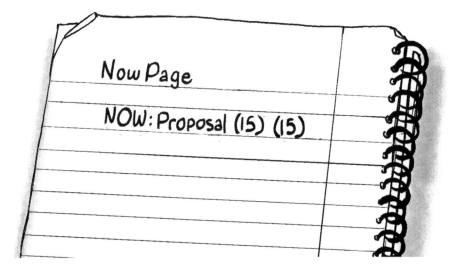

Beep! The time is up again. You successfully focused on the task for a total of 30 minutes by now.

Though you are not yet finished, you decide to switch to another task. You draw an arrow by the task to indicate that you are not yet done, and start on a new task.

Now Page

↱ NOW: Proposal (15) (15)
NOW: Review training (15)

Let's say you finish the new task within the allotted 15 minutes, so you check it off.

Now, you decide to take a break. Since you are no longer working on a task, you write

OFF: Break

Now Page

↱ NOW: Proposal (15) (15)
✔ NOW: Review training (15)

OFF: Break

You could be even more specific about your break activity. Here are some suggestions:

OFF: Stretching

OFF: Socializing

OFF: Volleyball

The activity name for the OFF tag is optional.

The OFF: tag should be applied to any activity that you do not want to be on the clock, or activities that are more collaborative, in which you do not have full control of the activity agenda, such as a meeting. Here are other variations of the OFF tag

OFF: Meeting

OFF: Call

OFF: Think

During your OFF time, if you find yourself inadvertently working on a task, simply start a NOW tag for that task. No task is too small for the NOW tag.

# Deeper Meaning

The NOW tag prompts us to consciously choose what we work on. This conscious choice is crucial. This, as journalist and meditation practitioner Dan Harris asserts, is a critical part of being mindful as it allows you to work assertively rather than reactively.[10] It calls for active thinking as opposed to randomly undertaking whichever task that shows up on our doorstep, or following the path of least resistance. When we write down the NOW tag and the task name, we are setting the stake in the ground, indicating that we are now focusing our mind and our energy on this task. Nothing is more crucial than consciously choosing what we work on. After all, the tasks that we engage in determine the results that we get.

_____

[10] Harris, Dan. 10% Happier: How I Tamed the Voice in My Head, Reduced Stress without Losing My Edge, and Found Self-help That Actually Works: A True Story.

The NOW tag also serves as a written documentation of the chosen task. If we were to make this choice mentally, it would be easy to forget that we made this choice or be tempted to switch to a different task with little accountability. The NOW tag serves as a persistent reminder and a sign of accountability.

The NOW tag also signifies that we have given ourselves the permission to fully focus on this task. Permission granted, the nagging thoughts about other tasks that are outstanding can rest and allow us to be fully engaged in our NOW task.

In terms of the 15-minute timeframe, it comprises a digestible and realistic chunk of time. It is a known quantity. Even if the task is difficult or boring, just knowing that you will only have to endure it for 15 minutes, makes it more bearable and who knows, maybe even pleasant or, do I dare say, exciting! The typically exaggerated fear that we would be "totally consumed by this task forever" suddenly vanishes.

You are now in the magical world of "focus!" Your senses, your thoughts, your feelings, and your actions are centered on the one and only

NOW task. Now is your opportunity to make real progress. The actions you take on the NOW task are most noteworthy because once we start to take action, our confidence and motivation go up, and our stress level goes down.

The 15-minute timeframe also serves as a checkpoint. It is an opportunity for a course correction. Are we on the right track? If so, we can choose to keep going for another 15 minutes. Are we no longer productive? If so, it is probably time to switch, perhaps to one of the urgent items that we deferred earlier.

Furthermore, the users of the Perfect Day Method reported that they not only became more aware of time and how much time they were spending on their tasks, but also their ability to estimate the length of time it would take to complete their tasks improved significantly—all valuable skills in the workplace and beyond.

The NOW tag and the 15-minute timeframe can also be described as your path to being mindful of the present moment and making the most out of it, 15 minutes at a time.

# Discoveries

When you first begin using the Perfect Day Method you may find that you overestimate how much you can accomplish in a day. This may be because you do not realize how much uninterrupted time you actually have to sit and work on your tasks, or how long a particular task actually takes. As you will see, the journal will help inform you of how your time is spent and help you make better estimations over time.

Meanwhile, you will also be surprised at how much you can accomplish in a focused 15 minutes! When you put your mind to it - that is, by setting an intention "NOW:" to work on one task for a quantified amount of time (15) - your focus seems to slow time and multiply your productivity. This is a particularly welcome discovery to those with busy schedules and only bits of time here and there to work:

*"[One of the top three benefits I received was a] reduced mental concept that "I don't have time to do that"* --Gary McLeod

*"In the time between meetings, I have used this method to become more productive and chisel away at my tasks. I have found that little by little, my effort has increased my efficiency substantially and no time is wasted!"* -- Katie Uckele

# Chapter 4

# The E-mail Task

# How it Works

E-mail messages that *ping* into our inboxes are often the cause of distraction and eventual frustration when we try to promptly read and answer e-mails while also trying to work on a task. Rather than letting our inbox drive our attention and pull us in different directions, let's treat e-mail as a task. Read on to learn how to handle your e-mail inbox in bulk and subdue the headache of e-mails.

# Treat E-mail as a Task

What does it mean to treat e-mail as a task? What are the characteristics of a task that we want to borrow and apply to e-mail? Here they are:

1. A task has a clear beginning
2. A task has a clear ending
3. A task has a process or a structure that we can follow

When you start to work on e-mail, use the NOW tag on the NOW Page to indicate clearly that you started the e-mail task (*this is your clear beginning*):

NOW: E-mail (15)

Then, when the 15 minutes are up, you can decide either to continue working on the e-mail task or to end the e-mail task (*with a clear ending*).

During the e-mail task, you follow a process and therefore optimize how you manage your e-mail as explained below.

# The e-mail task process[11]

Opening our inbox is like opening a Pandora's box of distractions, so let's learn the techniques for quickly processing our inbox. We want to respond to the urgent messages immediately, and quickly organize the rest of the messages by priority with as little effort as possible.

Your e-mail client should allow you to setup categories, labels, or tags for your e-mails. We suggest creating three of these:

- Today
- Tomorrow
- Waiting For

---

[11] Extracted from The Accomplishing More With Less Workbook, and the Accomplishing More With Google Apps book

When you process your inbox (going from most recent at top to least recent at bottom), quickly examine each message and ask yourself, "do I want to handle this message now or not?"

This appears to be a trivial or obvious question. However, it is a crucial part of being purposeful, not getting lost in e-mails just because they happen to be in your inbox, and not being slowed down by indecision. Repeat after me: "do I want to handle this message now or not?"

If this message is urgent, or can be responded to quickly and easily, then the answer is likely to be yes ("I want to respond now"), so respond and remove it from your inbox. If the answer is no ("I don't want to respond now"), then decide which category to assign it to. For e-mails that you would like to handle later today, assign these to the "Today" category. For e-mails that do not need to be handled today, assign these to the "Tomorrow" category. For e-mails that you decide to delegate but want to keep an eye on, assign these to "Waiting For." For e-mails that don't require an action, but may be needed later for future reference, simply file these away.

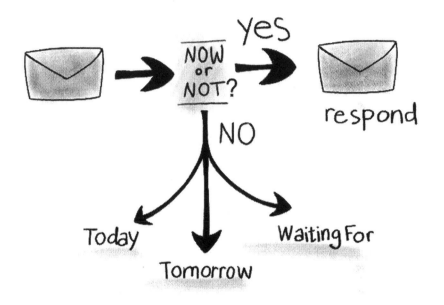

# Revisiting e-mail by category

Aside from the e-mail task described above, which needs to be done periodically during the day, you also need to revisit the Today category, once or more during the day, to process these e-mails by the end of the day, in which case you would note:

NOW: E-mail Today (15)

In addition, you also need to revisit the Tomorrow and Waiting For categories once a day, in which case you would note:

NOW: E-mail Tomorrow (15)

NOW: E-mail Waiting For (15)

As you may have noticed by now, whenever we tackle a task, the more specific we are about the task we are working on the better. There are several tasks that we have identified within the process of handling e-mail. There is the processing of your inbox, and there is the handling of e-mails within their respective categories - Today, Tomorrow, and Waiting For. Each task is tagged differently in the NOW page as indicated above.

Later in the book, we tackle the end-of-day reconciliation process to provide more insights on the timing of these tasks.

# Deeper Meaning

When uncontrolled, e-mail can take over our workday. As Parkinson's Law says, work expands so as to fill the time available for its completion. This is so true of e-mail. We can literally spend all day doing e-mail and many people do. Remember that e-mail is everyone else's priorities. When we are consumed by e-mail, we are not likely to be focused on our core priorities. The opportunity cost of e-mail is enormous.

E-mail can also be a constant interruption, keeping us in the "chaos" zone, where not only we are operating at 10% capacity, but we are getting hyper, agitated, and scattered.

When we treat e-mail as a task, we contain e-mail instead of it controlling us. The e-mail task prompts us to follow a specific process, and quickly move from one e-mail to the next, instead of addressing one e-mail at a time, every few minutes, all day long. The e-mail task keeps us aware of how much time we spend on e-mail and prevents us from getting bogged down with uncertainty and indecisiveness.

The e-mail task as defined in the Perfect Day Method helps us tame e-mail and transform it into an amazing tool, as it was intended to be. E-mail is really an important digital communication tool that gives us control of our collaborative process. As communications expert Dawna Ballard describes it, this type of interaction gives us more control over our time than traditional forms of communication by allowing us to decide whether or not we will collaborate at a given moment.[12]

---

[12] "Finding Balance in an Age of Always-On Business: The Time-Space Mixtape" by Dawna Ballard

# Discoveries

Handling e-mail as a task illustrates one of the essential goals of the Perfect Day Method, that is, to actively decide what you are doing, rather than allow yourself to be swept along by the tides of work. Many of us feel so obliged to prioritize others - to respond to our colleagues immediately, to report to our bosses right away - that we lose sense of our priorities. By handling e-mail on your own terms, on the basis of your priorities (see your TODAY page), you can reclaim control of your workday. This, ultimately, makes both you and your team happy.

*"It did help to consciously recognize when I was being interrupted and that I had a choice to deal with now or add to a list--and that I needed to make a choice rather than be swept along. ... It was also extremely helpful to ID email as a task and only look at it when I was intending to. Overall, I felt much more focused all day, much more quickly able to resume something if I was*

*interrupted (either by someone else or by my own thoughts), and it was a day when I felt I got a lot done."* -- Valerie Gilbert

# Chapter 5

# MicroPlanning™

# How it Works

MicroPlanning™ is a very useful technique for making the most of a focus session. Many of us may simply dive into a task blindly, only to be stalled when we realize we skipped a step and need to first download a program, get information from a co-worker, or consult our boss. Alternatively, some of us may dawdle or procrastinate when we do not know exactly what needs to be done or exactly how to do it.

When we create a Micro-Plan we list the key steps needed to complete the task at hand. Doing so requires us to think and figure out exactly how we will accomplish a task. Breaking a task down like this helps make a task more approachable and manageable. MicroPlanning™ also helps us to quickly return to a task after an interruption and know where we left off.

Tasks that involve several steps and have some level of complexity or irregularity are better candidates for MicroPlanning™.

# Create Your Micro-Plan™

When you are about to embark on a task with multiple steps, you can briefly outline the key steps needed below the NOW: Task (15). You don't need to write down all the steps in full detail, just enough to keep you on track as you progress. Ideally the MicroPlan™ is handwritten in just a minute or two.

Then as you work on the task, check off steps as you complete them. This way if you are to be interrupted in mid-task you will know where you left off.

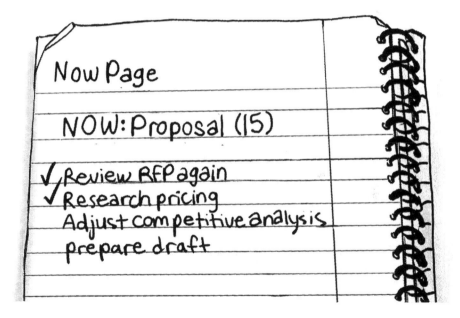

Often as we work on a task, unanticipated steps and new ideas come to mind. This is totally fine. Simply add new steps and related ideas into the MicroPlan™ under the task so you do not forget them or let them derail your focus.

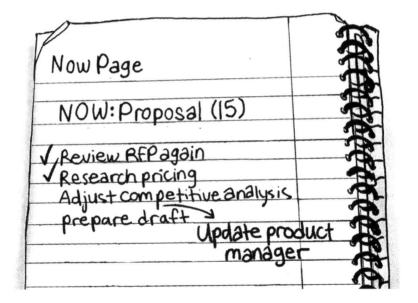

# Deeper Meaning

Taking a task or an issue and breaking it down into smaller steps can help manage it better and reduce related stress. We generally do this when managing projects or larger tasks, but not typically for smaller tasks. MicroPlanning™ consists of breaking down even small tasks, like the NOW task, into small steps. The MicroPlan™ gives us a "visual map" of where we are headed. If we don't complete all the steps within the MicroPlan™ within the 15-minute timeframe, we can continue for another 15 minutes. If, however, we decide to switch to another task for now, and get back to the MicroPlanned task later, when it is time to get back to it, we have the steps we need to make the return seamless and effortless.

When we are working on the MicroPlan, and if new ideas about new steps come up, we add them to the MicroPlan. The MicroPlan is indeed fluid. It continues to evolve as we work on the task. The MicroPlan frees up our short-term memory from having to hold on to the original steps and the additional steps, therefore reducing the risk of losing them and reducing the potential overload. This is enormous because our short-term memory is limited in capacity. Without the help of the MicroPlan, our memory is easily overwhelmed, causing us stress.

MicroPlanning also enables us to achieve sharp focus. With the MicroPlan, we are not just focused on the task at hand, we are focused on a specific step within the task. This is sharp focus that enables us to tap into our creativity and strategic thinking, resulting in innovative solutions instead of quick-fixes.

Finally, and most importantly in today's world of distractions and interruptions, the MicroPlan is our rescuer when it comes to task switching. If we have to switch to a different task, whether voluntarily or when we get pulled into a new task as a result of external demands, when we return to the MicroPlan, it serves as a visual map that can help us regain context and get re-orientated quickly and effortlessly, hence turning us into remarkable multi-taskers. Therefore MicroPlanning is the solution to today's dilemma, which is the need to be skilled at focusing and getting meaningful results accomplished, and the need to be able to manage multiple tasks and demands when we are confronted with them!

# Discoveries

While utilizing this method, you will discover more about yourself and your work-style. In particular, you may find that you are either

A. someone who likes to write things down and plan out details, or
B. someone who likes to see the big picture and dislikes getting caught up in planning details

Understandably, many big-picture and intuitive people find the method more challenging to adopt. If this is you, you may find the method helpful in balancing your weakness for organizing and planning details. This, as it so happens, helps you to better see the bigger picture. Micro-Planning, especially, helps you visualize what you are trying to achieve and how you will achieve it.

Meanwhile, detail-oriented people who already write things down are quick to adopt the method. They find it helps them feel more organized and in control, and they enjoy having a record of their day to evaluate.

However, this can become burdensome if the detail-oriented allow themselves to get consumed in trying to record and write everything down. If this is you, don't feel that you must micro-manage and record the minutiae of every minute. Remember that the Perfect Day Method is a tool for you to use to help, not hinder, your productivity.

# Chapter 6

# Thoughts about

# Things to Do

# How it Works

One of the most common thoughts that interrupt us in the middle of a task is a thought about something to do - call a vendor, forward meeting notes, update a computer program. Depending on the task, some of us may be tempted to do it right away; some of us may brush the thought aside for later only to remember again when we are in the middle of the next task.

In a Perfect Day we choose to refocus on the task at hand - at least for the remainder of our current 15-minute increment. However, we don't want to forget about the to-do item, and we also don't want to leave it floating around in our minds, continually distracting us. So we write it down. Where? The journal, of course! Again the journal saves us in its simplicity and accessibility. Rather than opening up your note-taking application or calendar app and risking further distraction, jot it down in the journal right beside you.

# Where to Write New Tasks

Depending on the timeframe of the to-do item in question, you have three options for where you can write it in the journal. Remember that you have three main pages in the journal, so you can either jot it down on the TODAY page, the CAPTURE page, or in a "Next" column on your NOW page that we will shortly explain.

Here are the guidelines:

- Next Column: If you'd like to tackle this task next, or soon after your current task, write it in the Next Column.
- TODAY page: If you'd like to complete this task sometime today, add it to the TODAY page.
- CAPTURE page: If you're not sure when you'd like to address this task, and/or you don't want to spend too much time figuring it out right now, put it on the CAPTURE page.

# The Next Column

The Next Column is a miniature to-do list we add in the margin of our NOW page. When an urgent task comes up that we'd like to get to soon then we create a Next Column and write it there. Notice, as illustrated below, the Next Column is simply your own handwritten side bar; it doesn't need to look a certain way. It's a section where we can add more urgent to-do's so it's the first thing we see when we return to the journal.

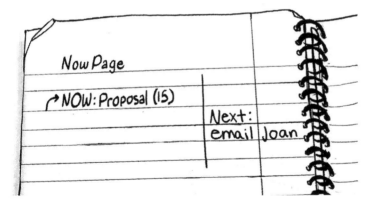

# Adding to the TODAY Page

When a new task comes up that we would like to get done sometime today, though not necessarily right away, you can add this to your TODAY page.

# Adding to the Capture Page

When thoughts about things-to-do interrupt us in the middle of a focus session, the CAPTURE page is our default catch-all page. If you have any doubt about whether this task belongs in a Next Column or the TODAY page, don't spend any more time and effort deciding. Simply put it on your CAPTURE page and stay focused on the task at hand!

Capture Page

- Planning a talent show for the offsite

# Deeper Meaning

Our mind tends to be busy in the background with myriad of thoughts continuously popping up about, well you name it. We remember things that we need to do, we have ideas related to projects we are working on, we cycle through old situations and events, we imagine future ones, just to name a few.

Thoughts about things to do are especially distracting because we tend to jump into these things right away especially those that appear to be urgent (typically perceived urgency) or minor (we can get them done quickly and out of the way) or enticing for one reason or another. Other thoughts may not tempt us, but they continue to weigh in the back of our minds, wasting cognitive energy.

For instance, many thoughts of things to do come from unfinished tasks. This is due to what is known in psychology as the Zeigarnik effect. Psychologist Bluma Zeigarnik observed that people are better to recall interrupted tasks than completed tasks. She concluded that "the lack of closure [of an unfinished task] promotes some continued task-related cognitive effort, accompanied by a preservation of task-related memory traces and thus a tendency for task components to be retained in memory."[13] In other words, pending items weigh on our minds and can take away part of our focus on the task at hand.

In the Perfect Day however, we make a note of all such thoughts in designated areas in the journal, and resume our focus on the NOW task.

The skill of intercepting a thought, before we act on it, needs to be learned and practiced. This technique is designed to "prevent the voice in your head from leading you around by the nose," as Dan Harris puts it. The Perfect Day Method enables you to learn and practice this skill naturally. Having a clearly defined NOW task, having the 15-minute clock ticking and

---

[13] Greist-Bousquet, S., Schiffman, N. (1992). The effect of Task interruption and closure on perceived duration. Bulletin of the Psychonomic Society, 30(1), 9-11.

therefore your awareness of time heightened, and having designated areas for capturing the thoughts about the to-do items, all work together to make it possible for us to intercept these thoughts and channel them appropriately instead of getting off track.

Another factor that comes into play here is the enormous temptation that some of these interrupting thoughts and to-do items offer, especially when we work on a difficult task, a boring task, or a mandatory task where we have little choice. While the Perfect Day Method aspects mentioned above (the NOW task, the 15-minute timer, and the designated areas for capturing items) offer great shields against the temptation, the biggest protection of all however is a whole other aspect of the Perfect Day Method that we haven't touched upon yet—which should come at no surprise if you have already tried the method as you go through this book. This aspect is the amazing feeling of fulfillment and accomplishment that you experience when you focus and get deep into your task, experience being fully present, and accomplish a meaningful outcome. Once you experience this feeling, the Perfect Day is yours!

# Discoveries

Notice that the TODAY page is allowed to grow organically with your day. We know that with all our intentions and goal settings, unexpected situations arise, news arrives in our inbox, crises call in to our office. This means that you do not need to exhaustively list everything you would like to accomplish when you begin the journal for the day. Leave room for the unexpected.

# Chapter 7

# Thoughts and Emotions

# How it Works

We all know how difficult it is to leave our personal problems at home (and our work problems at work). Throughout the workday, we experience so many thoughts and emotions, many that only add to our stress. Worries, hang-ups, anxiety, and unresolved problems plague our minds, preventing us from fully focusing on our work. Worse, many of these negativities may slip by unnoticed, becoming the background noise in our heads and discoloring our day.

# Managing Negative Thoughts and Emotions in the Journal

In a Perfect Day, instead of letting ourselves stew in negative thoughts and emotions, we acknowledge them, label them, and move beyond them. Science has shown that if you label an emotion or thought, it helps your brain contain it and prevents you from blowing it out of proportion. The process of managing negative thoughts and emotions involves three steps:

1. First we identify the thought or emotion.
2. Then we rank it. This helps us be realistic about how bad the situation is, if it is even bad at all.
3. Lastly, we accept it and move on--or when appropriate, we might engage into actively addressing it as explained in the subsequent chapter.

For negative thoughts, use the following notation in your journal:

THOUGHT: [Label or description], [rank], [action]

The suggested ranking is a 1 to 10 scale, where 1 is the most troublesome and 10 is the happiest.

The action can be simply to accept the feeling at this point and resume the task at hand--or to take some additional steps which is a topic discussed in the Deeper Meaning section below.

For instance, as you work on a difficult proposal, your self-dialogue may kick in whispering "you're not good at this" and starting to distract you.

You might then note it on your NOW page:

We deal the same way with emotions using the EMOTION: tag:

Now Page

NOW: Proposal (15)
EMOTION: Anxiety, 5, okay

Accepting => Freeing

Ranking => Realistic

Labeling => Containing

# Think Positively: Acknowledge Your Accomplishments

Now that we've dealt with your negative thoughts and emotions, we want to encourage positive ones. One way to do this is to remember to acknowledge your accomplishments. So often we accomplish one thing, and look immediately towards the next task at hand. Work begins to look like an endless to-do list, the never-ending grind. By remembering to acknowledge your accomplishments, work becomes much more enjoyable and rewarding.

So now, when you complete a task, no matter how small, take a moment to acknowledge this in your journal. Let yourself enjoy the satisfaction of drawing a check-mark by a completed task and throw a mini-celebration. :)

Now Page

NOW: Proposal (15)

- ✓ Review RFP again
- ✓ Research pricing
- ✓ Adjust competitive analysis
- ✓ prepare draft

YAY!!

# Deeper Meaning

Thoughts aren't limited to things to do. Our mind is capable of creating a wide range of thoughts about the events and situations that we experience, ranging from interpretations of what happened, to assumptions related to what happened, opinions about what happened, and more thoughts about what might have happened, or what might happen in the future. Similarly, we experience feelings about these events and situations including fears and anxieties about past, current, or future events or issues.

Some of these thoughts and feelings tend to be distorted and therefore largely interfere with our ability to accomplish things and be happy. As Dan Harris describes, "Thoughts calcify into opinions, little seeds of discontent blossom into bad moods, unnoticed back pain makes me inexplicably irritable with anyone who happens to cross my path." If we repress these thoughts and emotions, indicates Alicia Ruelaz Maher M.D.[14], cortisol remains at high levels causing a decrease in immunity and making us more vulnerable to injury, just to highlight one of the many effects that distorted thoughts and feelings can have on us. In addition, the underlying issues won't go away when we repress them. If we act out these thoughts and emotions instead of repressing them, this is not likely to help either because it may lead to a whole new set of problems including disagreements and conflicts, not to mention physical harm. So what do we do with these thoughts and feelings?

The answer is simple but requires some practice in mindfulness:

First we must become aware of the emotion. Google's meditation leader Chade-Meng Tan suggests that the best way to do this is to turn our attention to the body. This is because every emotion is experienced by the body just as much as it is in the mind. When we are nervous or excited, we

---

14 Alicia Ruelaz Maher M.D. Author of From Scattered to Centered: Understanding and Transforming the Distracted Brain

may notice our heart rate accelerates and palms get sweaty. When we are embarrassed or angry we may notice that heat rises to our cheeks. Simply observing these bodily sensations and their effect allows us to better manage our emotions.

Second, we label the thought or feeling. A study in the journal Psychological Science[15] demonstrated how labeling feelings can alter their impact on us. Researchers put people into a scanner that revealed which part of their brains were active as the researchers showed them photographs. When the photographs were of angry or fearful stimuli, the instinctual, reactive part of their brains would light up. The researchers then had these subjects do a mindfulness practice for several weeks. Whenever the subjects noticed anger or fear, they would label it "This is anger", "This is fear". When the researchers tested them again with the same photographs, they found that a different part of the brain was now

---

15 Extracted from article written by Alicia Ruelaz Maher M.D. in the Less is More Blog (www.people-onthego.com/blog)

lighting up. Now, angry and fearful photographs were activating the higher order parts of the brain, the part associated with thinking in words about emotional experiences. So, instead of experiencing reactivity upon these stimuli, their brains were now taking a step back from it. You can imagine the profound advantage of this change. When stimuli activate this part of the brain, you can choose an effective response, rather than just react.

This is exactly what the Perfect Day Method is training us to do. By labeling thoughts and feelings, and therefore giving them words, we are training ourselves to respond differently, activating the higher order parts of the brain, and therefore being calmer and more logical, instead of reactive.

After we label the thought or emotion, we rank it, then either accept it and move on, or when possible and appropriate, replace it by a more realistic thought.

Ranking the thought or feeling is intended to help us be more realistic, as opposed to having an exaggerated reaction to our experiences. The mere action of stopping and ranking the thought or feeling, already engages the higher order parts of the brain, and therefore engages our wisdom. This is in and by itself a significant improvement. Then, as we attempt to rank the situation, for most situations, it is likely that we conclude that the situation is not as horrific as it may have initially "felt." The daily situations that seem to be horrifying are more likely to be the creation of our own imagination. Even if the situation happens to be a difficult one, once we engage our rational thinking, it is likely that we get into problem solving and action instead of fear and paralysis. As Chade-Meng Tan suggests, assess your situation according to these principles "1. Know when you are not in pain. 2. Do not feel bad about feeling bad. 3. Do not feed the monsters. 4. Start every thought with kindness and humor."

After all, we are human beings and over our lifetime, we are going to experience thousands or even millions of thoughts and feelings. This is a fact! Recognizing and acknowledging this fact, instead of persistently resisting it and punishing ourselves, and/or others, for having these thoughts and feelings, is an essential step in moving beyond them.

There is more that we can do after the labeling, ranking, and accepting. Dr. Albert Ellis, in his book, *How to Refuse to Make Yourself Miserable About Anything, Yes Anything!* refers to "disputing" the underlying beliefs which are the root cause for our stress and overwhelm, and replacing them by more realistic ones. Dr. David Burns, in his book, *Feeling Good*, talks about 10 distortions that are common in our thinking. Once we become more adept at identifying them, we can relinquish them and enjoy a more positive experience. Later in this book, we discuss The Awareness Wheel, which is a tool that can help us work through the thoughts and feelings skillfully.

While there is more that we can do after the labeling, ranking, and accepting, as described above, it may not be practical or possible to do this on the spot in the midst of a busy day while handling urgent tasks. If this is the case, we can rely on the labeling, ranking, and accepting for now so we can move on and be productive again, and revisit the thought or feeing later when time allows.

The labeling, ranking, and accepting translates to an ability to focus, without repressing such thoughts and feelings, and feeling more content in the moment. Such moments incrementally lead to a happier you! Happiness is contagious and so a happier you will mean happier people around you and a happier workplace.

# Discoveries

As you may have noticed, a big part of the Perfect Day Method is about learning to be productive in a healthy and sustainable way. This means recognizing that we are not robots; we have a mental and physical well-being to keep in mind. Though we may feel the pressure to, we cannot and should not work non-stop. That is neither healthy nor productive. Instead, the Perfect Method teaches us to follow our natural rhythms of energy. As described in the Results Curve chapter, working productively means working in focused bursts of energy, regrouping to collaborate, and then stopping to play and recharge.

One of the biggest challenges many of our users face at work is remembering and allowing themselves to take a break. As a result, many face exhaustion and burnout by the end of the day. The Perfect Day Method makes it easier to give ourselves permission to stop since each focus session has a definitive end and a choice to resume, switch gears, or stop and take an "OFF:" break. Plus, when acknowledging how much we've accomplished, part of our mini-celebration should be taking a moment to breathe.

"At the end of a 15-minute time, I felt like moving ahead -- but I still needed the break so my body told me to take it -- and I would forget to put my timer on pause while I went to get some water, for example. In hindsight, that sense of permission is probably more important than whether I recorded NOW, Off, or Switch correctly." -- Linda Lingane

# Chapter 8

# The Awareness Wheel

# How it Works

When difficult situations come up, and negative thoughts and emotions persist, we need robust tools to handle them. Otherwise we get overwhelmed and highly distracted, all diminishing our ability to have 15 minutes of focus and get important accomplishments underway.

The Awareness Wheel is exactly that; a robust tool that you want at your disposal when difficult situations come up and/or when negative thoughts and emotions take over. It is a technique that was originally described by Sherod & Phyllis Miller (authors of "Core Communication, Skills and Processes") that can help us break a situation down into more manageable components, become aware of what is going on below the surface, and identify how best to handle it.

# The Five Components of the Awareness Wheel

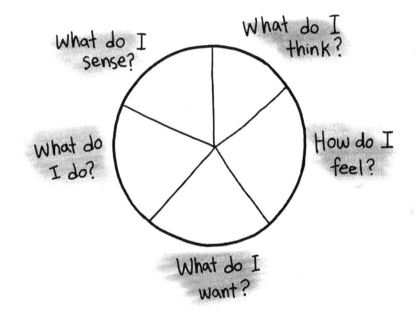

Each component presents a question, each question prompting us to think deeper, become more aware, and improve our ability to manage through the situation.

The five questions:

1. *What do I sense about the situation?* The point here is to identify the facts.
2. *What do I think about the situation?* This has to do with what is going on in our mind such as our interpretations, our assumptions, and our opinions.
3. *How do I feel about the situation?* This can range from extreme anger or fear on one end, to joy and happiness on the other end, and all shades in between.
4. *What do I want in this situation?* This has to do with reflecting on our purpose and what we want to accomplish.
5. *What do I do in this situation?* This has to do with identifying the potential actions and the best possible action.

This process is iterative. It may take several tries to uncover the underlying facts, thoughts, feelings, wants, and come up with notable actions. The following case study illustrates the process.

# The case study

Mark is unhappy at work and when asked to define the problem, here is how he put it: "My boss doesn't care about my professional development and I am really unhappy at work". This situation is very stressful for Mark and is taking up a lot of his energy. His working relationships are impacted, he is not feeling good at work and even outside work, and his performance is suffering. Let us see how the Awareness Wheel can help. We will demonstrate how a coach can help Mark use the Awareness Wheel to manage this situation:

Coach: "Mark, what happened?"

Mark: "She doesn't care"

Where does Mark's statement ("She doesn't care") fall in the Awareness Wheel? This is Mark's subjective view of what happened. This is clearly his interpretation of what happened. It is a thought. The coach makes a note of this in the Awareness Wheel, indicating to Mark that this is his interpretation, and repeats the question again:

Coach: "Tell me more about what actually happened?"

Mark: "She cancelled the meeting"

This is a fact. Mark reports real data. He saw (with his "senses") the meeting cancelled notice in his e-mail inbox. The coach takes note of this and proceeds to help Mark explore the feeling part:

Coach: "Mark, how do you feel about the meeting being cancelled?"

Mark: "I feel I am not important"

Even though Mark uses the words "I feel," the statement "I am not important" is more of an interpretation than a feeling. Using words such as "I feel" to express a thought is common. There might be a feeling associated with the thought, but that is something that would need to be explored. For now, the "I am not important" statement is noted as a thought. Now the coach tries to get to the feeling behind the thought.

Coach: "Mark, how else are you feeling about this?"

Mark pauses for a bit and then says: "I am sad and disappointed"

As you may have noticed already, the coach tends to repeat the same question more than once. The first time, he usually gets a reactionary answer such as "I feel that I am not important" and then the second time (or sometime third or fourth time) he gets more meaningful insights into what is really going on such as "I am sad and disappointed".

The coach continues to explore this area with Mark, and then when he thinks that Mark is ready to move to the next component, the coach makes an initial attempt at asking Mark about his wants.

Coach: "So what do you want Mark"

Mark: "I want to have the meeting"

Then Mark proceeds to say:

Mark: "I will tell her that I am unhappy".

Mark has just expressed an action here (not necessary the best action, but it is an action). The Coach notices that the want and action expressed by Mark are reactionary, so he asks Mark again about his thoughts and feelings about the situation, and gives him the opportunity to express these further and spend time exploring these. Then later in the conversation, the coach makes another attempt at asking Mark about what Mark really wants. Mark takes a deep breath at that point, and says:

Mark: "I want more recognition".

Then Mark adds: "I want input on my career development".

This is a big "Ah-Ha" moment for Mark! Mark just realized it is not the meeting that really got him emotionally mixed up and stressed, it is the underlying need to have recognition and the desire for a better career development plan that he seems to be missing at work. The meeting was just the tip of the iceberg and his reaction to the meeting being cancelled is just that, a reaction. This is one of the key purposes of the wheel – to facilitate the process of becoming more aware of the real causes behind what we are experiencing on the surface.

The coach is now ready to ask the important question:

Coach: "So what are you going to do about this situation Mark?"

Mark: "I will ask to reschedule the meeting and discuss the real issues with my boss"

Then Mark adds: "I will also find a coach or a mentor"

Another big "Ah-Ha"!

The Awareness Wheel helped transform this difficult situation (or even seemingly insurmountable situation in Mark's mind at the time when his judgment is impaired) into an actionable one. We started with "My boss doesn't care about my professional development and I am really unhappy at work" and ended up with a better understanding of the underlying needs and specific action items that can be carried out in order to get these underlying needs met. Nicely done!

The job is not done however. Mark still needs to implement these actions. As he implements the actions, he needs to watch for his interpretations and assumptions sneaking in again. If he continues practicing the Awareness Wheel each step of the way, he will continue to refine and enhance his actions. Soon he will become experienced at this tool and use it more naturally to help him through difficult situations. He is now on his way to discovering a whole new world of accomplishments.

# The Purpose of the Wheel

To start with, the simple act of defining the "issue" and getting engaged with the Awareness Wheel is in and of itself an empowering exercise. It puts our energy and creativity in motion. It helps us challenge the status quo and get busy with solutions – all essential to solving problems and feeling better. In addition, the Awareness Wheel serves several important purposes:

1. It helps us separate reality from imagination (facts from interpretations and assumptions)
2. It helps us separate thoughts from feelings (what the mind is creating, as opposed to how we are truly feeling)
3. It helps us identify our true wants (instead of our reactionary wants)
4. It facilitates identifying the best possible action
5. It enables us to positively influence the end results

In our daily work and personal life, the default sequence of events is that an event takes place in our environment for instance. we sense something (someone says or does something), we quickly interpret it in a certain way (unfortunately this may be the not-so-constructive way), we feel a certain way about it (not so positive feelings caused by not-so-constructive interpretations), and then act accordingly (poor action caused by this sequence). This whole sequence happens very quickly and transparently. We don't even notice it. It looks and feels as if we are just taking actions to deal with what happened, yet we wonder why we aren't getting the results we desire. The Awareness Wheel enables us to interfere and change this sequence. The end goal is significantly improved actions and results, not to mention breakthroughs!

# Self-Coaching

We presented the case study above by having a coach walk through the Awareness Wheel with Mark. While it would be ideal to have a coach help us along the way, more often than not, we need to be our own coach. The Awareness Wheel is the ideal tool for self-coaching.

The Awareness Wheel components and related questions are exactly the kind of questions we should ask ourselves. Writing down the answers, as we progress through the process, is critical. This helps us avoid "spinning our wheels" by reiterating the same thoughts and feelings endlessly. This will also help us detect "imbalance" (spending too much time and energy on one component of the wheel without paying enough attention to the rest). The Awareness Wheel is largely about balance. It helps bring to the forefront all aspects of a situation. It helps us have a more objective view of the world as opposed to getting too focused on one area and losing ourselves in it.

As we saw in the case study, it is important to repeat the same question more than once to get beyond the initial superficial answer. It usually takes several passes to get to the core issues. If you don't get to the desired results in one session, you may want to give yourself a break, let the issues percolate, and then resume later. This process of self-questioning and self-coaching is one of the most worthwhile activities we can undertake if we want to succeed, feel better, and accomplish more with less stress.

# Deeper Meaning

The Awareness Wheel provides a practical method for dealing with what otherwise can be vague and complex aspects of our being. We already revealed above when we discussed thoughts and emotions, how putting words behind thoughts and feelings was proven to activate the higher order parts of the brain, and therefore helping us become calmer and more logical instead of reactive. The Awareness Wheel is a structured approach for doing exactly that and a lot more than that. It also guides us in reviewing the facts, better examine our wants and needs, formulate and take action. This is accomplished iteratively allowing us to go deeper and discover hidden beliefs, fears, and desires, but most importantly get to a closure on the issues whenever possible.

To better grasp the potential life changing benefits of practicing the Awareness Wheel, let us explore the work of Carol Dweck, Ph.D., who is a Stanford professor and who spent years researching why some people fulfill their potential and why some don't. Her findings point out that when people believe that their basic traits are fixed, which she refers to as "fixed mindset," they limit themselves and create obstacles that stand in the way of their success and happiness. On the other hand, when people believe that their qualities are things that they can develop, which she refers to as "growth mindset," they learn and achieve and pave the road to fulfillment.

In her book *Mindset: The New Psychology of Success*[16], Dr. Dweck provides a simple assessment to help determine if one has a fixed or growth mindset by asking which of these statements you mostly agree with:

---

16 Carol Dweck, Ph.D., Mindset: The New Psychology of Success (New York: Random House, 2006)

1. Your intelligence is something basic about you that you can't change very much

2. You can learn new things, but you can't really change how intelligent you are

3. No matter how much intelligence you have, you can always change it quite a bit

4. You can always substantially change how intelligent you are

Statements 1 and 2 indicate a fixed mindset, while statements 3 and 4 indicate a growth mindset. It is possible to display both mindsets, but most people lean towards one or the other. You could also substitute "artistic talent," "sports ability," or "business skill," for "intelligence" in the above statements and assess your mindset in these areas.

It is not only your abilities; it is also your personal qualities that can be in question. Dr. Dweck proceeds to provide yet another assessment related to personal qualities by asking with which of these statements do you mostly agree:

1. You are a certain kind of person, and there is not much that can be done to change that
2. No matter what kind of person you are, you can always change substantially
3. You can do things differently, but the important parts of who you are can't really be changed.
4. You can always change basic things about the kind of person you are

Statements 1 and 3 reflect the fixed mindset statements; 2 and 4 reflect the growth mindset. Which statement did you agree with? Does your mindset here differ from your intelligent mindset?

Beware, however. It is tempting to quickly conclude that you have a growth mindset. The real test is not our perception of our mindset but our behaviors and the impact we have on our surroundings. Here are a few more questions that I suggest you consider:

1. When was the last time you felt stressed and overwhelmed, and how did you deal with the situation? Did you feel

threatened, helpless, and/or impatient? Or did you soon confront the situation and work your way through it, in spite of the uncertainty and discomfort?

2. When was the last time you felt defensive? And how far did you go in defending yourself? Or did you acknowledge your part in the situation and move into resolving it constructively?

3. When was the last time you reflected closely on how others perceive you and paid attention to the impact you have on others? Did you seek feedback from others or did you ignore any signs of trouble or even justify them?

4. When was the last time you took on a new initiative, activity, or task that was not necessarily easy and didn't essentially match your natural strengths? Did you challenge the status quo and venture into expanding your horizon? Or did you stick to what you know and what you are good at?

5. What would others say if they were asked about whether you have a fixed or growth mindset? Would you dare to ask them?

As a result of your mindset, there are particular thoughts and behaviors that you are likely to experience. If you have a fixed mindset, you find it difficult to cope with challenges and especially with failures. You are overly concerned about how you will be judged, and you don't take risks. You value innate talent and capabilities but not effort. Overall, the fixed mindset is limiting and likely to create more stress, especially during challenging times.

If you have a growth mindset, you view challenges and failures as opportunities to learn. This doesn't necessarily make challenges and failures easy or desirable, but it does help you work your way through them and learn and develop as a result. Having a growth mindset, you value effort and take risks. The growth mindset is fulfilling and likely to create more calm and resolve during challenging times.

Dr. Dweck indicates that research shows that the most basic components of intelligence and personality traits can be changed, which supports the premise of the growth mindset. This is related to the concept of neuroplasticity, which I will discuss later in the book when it comes to stress management and which states that our brain is changeable. Therefore the good news: You can change your mindset through a practice of awareness and effort.

How? You guessed it! The Awareness Wheel practice is all about awareness and effort, thus helping you develop your growth mindset further, or, if you happen to be caught in the fixed mindset, giving you the opportunity to switch to the growth mindset. As meditation writer Dan Harris advises, "If you don't waste your energy on variables you cannot influence, you can focus much more effectively on those you can." With this attitude, you may undertake challenges that seemed previously unattainable. In the 15-minute timeframe, this translates to less background anxiety, less distracting thoughts and feelings, and increased ability to focus and be present, and experience these happy moments, which add up to a happier life!

# Discoveries

Users often find the Awareness Wheel practice useful in dealing with interpersonal conflicts at work. We each bring to the workplace our own way of doing things, our own ideas of how things are and how things should be, and these shape our perceptions often without us realizing it. As illustrated in the case study with Mark, we are quick to jump from observation, to interpretation, to feeling an emotion that can continue to influence our perception. Running our thoughts through the Awareness Wheel forces us to slow down and see the gaps in our thinking, the assumptions we made, and the possibilities we didn't consider. Rather than letting our thoughts control us, we can step back and analyze them. The Awareness Wheel is really a tool for mindfulness!

# Chapter 9

# External Interruptions

# How it Works

## Small versus Big Interruptions

Let's say we are in the middle of our task and Jane steps into the office to ask us about an issue that we are able to quickly resolve. It wasn't a long discussion, nor very distracting, and we are able to jump right back into our task afterwards. In this case, we'd simply make a note of this interruption and resume our 15-minute focus session.

This may be noted using her name, or a label identifying the issue, in parenthesis in line with the NOW task as shown here:

Now Page

NOW: Proposal (15)(Jane)

✓ Review RFP again
✓ Research pricing
Adjust competitive analysis
prepare draft → Update product
manager

However, what if Jane has an issue that requires substantial effort on our part, and as a result, we find ourselves working with Jane on this issue and taking our focus completely away from our original task? This qualifies as a "big" interruption. In this case, we acknowledge this change in focus by indicating on the NOW page that we have switched from our original task, and start a new NOW tag for the task that we are engaged in with Jane:

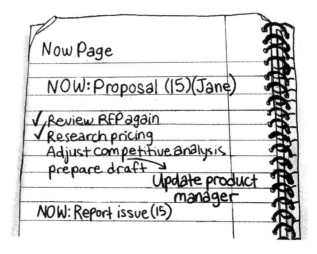

# Deeper Meaning

Most of us do not work alone. While working in an office or with a team, colleagues and other stakeholders may stop by your desk to ask a question or reach you otherwise, to discuss a project, or simply to have a friendly chat. This is not unwelcome, but it can be a distraction when you are in the middle of a focus session and not yet ready to collaborate or socialize.

As we discussed in the Results Curve™ chapter, we work most effectively when we give ourselves time to work individually in the Accomplishment Zone, then time to work together in the Collaboration Zone, and then socialize or take energizing breaks in the Play Zone. It's important to make sure you get enough focus time in your workday;

research has shown that people are more productive after having sufficient quiet time that permits no interruptions, digital or non-digital.[17]

There are ways to signal to your colleagues that you are busy - a closed office door, headphones, or a Do Not Disturb sign. And there are ways to negotiate your focus time with persistent colleagues - almost anything can wait 15 minutes!

Where you work – in a cubicle, an office, or a communal space - is also a factor of how often you may be interrupted. Studies have shown that "collocated" people who work near each other experience more interruptions as opposed to "distributed" people working in a more isolated environment.[18] They are also less likely to resume a task after interruption on their own initiative. This is a good reminder that your

---

[17] "Finding Balance in an Age of Always-On Business: The Time-Space Mixtape" by Dawna Ballard

[18] Gloria Mark, Victor M. Gonzalez, and Justin Harris "No Task Left Behind? Examining the Nature of Fragmented Work" (2005)

focus zone and collaborative zone need to be distinguished and communicated to your colleagues.

That said, not all interruptions are made equal. As previously discussed, "large" interruptions take us away from the task at hand and require us to switch our focus. Less "interruptive" interruptions may possibly benefit you if they are related to your current task. It may be helpful to let your colleagues know what you are working on and what sort of interruptions you are willing to allow.

However, some interruptions are too urgent or difficult to dismiss such as those relating to urgent customer issues for instance. When our 15-minute focus session is interrupted, noting interruptions down in your journal helps you become more aware of them, see clearly just how many (or how few) external interruptions you have on a daily basis, and the people and issues instigating these interruptions. This enables you to analyze these interruptions and explore strategic ways to minimize them or eradicate them at the root cause level. This will also help you better understand and plan your focus time, and potentially negotiate your focus time with colleagues.

MicroPlanning™ remains your best friend when it comes to managing interruptions. It enables you to handle interruptions like never before and stay fully productive. You create your MicroPlan™ for your NOW task. When you are interrupted by an urgent task, you switch to the new NOW task, and if applicable, start a MicroPlan™ for it. If you are interrupted again by yet another even more urgent task, you switch again, possibly creating a new MicroPlan™. With these MicroPlans™ at your fingertips, you can maneuver skillfully through the most demanding situations, and declare victory over interruptions and multi-tasking!

# Discoveries

I mentioned above that there are ways to signal to your colleagues that you are busy - a closed office door, headphones, or a Do Not Disturb sign. This may be a good start. However, to come up with meaningful ways for teams to minimize their interruptions to each other, some additional team discussions and agreements need to take place.

In one of our design thinking workshops[19], we asked teams to work together and come up with methods for helping each other stay focused, minimize interruptions, and yet stay responsive. Here is what one team (who called itself iFocus and rightfully so) came up with.

---

[19] Design Thinking to Focus, Collaborate, and Play workshop is a one-day workshop offered by People-OnTheGo

The iFocus team created a physical sign that was simply a whiteboard listing workers' names, their availability status (focused or collaborative and until what time), and a third column for workers to leave messages for their colleagues who are focused. This whiteboard would be posted at the entrance of the office, ideally a smaller office where workers know each other's names. The iFocus team debated whether the system should require workers to update their times of availability, or non-availability. They decided to leave this up to the worker because they didn't want to require the board to be rigorously updated. Instead it should be a tool for those who are busy and do not want to be interrupted. As they demonstrated, the system works when workers respect the board by checking it, and when workers who are busy (i.e. wanting to be focused and not interrupted) update it.

The iFocus team was very excited about their second solution, a computer and mobile application that is a digital version of the whiteboard system, and more. This application would list the team individuals and their availability, and would have a very visual user interface - each team member would be represented by a cartoon avatar, and the color of their box would signify if they were busy or available. If they were busy, there would be a mail icon for workers to leave a busy colleague a message. Again, the iFocus team did not want to require this app to be a chore to update. The best solution should automatically detect if a user is in focus mode or collaboration. The team was familiar with web apps that block distracting sites for a set time. They decided the iFocus computer app would do just that - when users wants to focus, they could disable certain programs and sites for a determined amount of time. The iFocus app would then automatically update their status as "busy" during this time. This solution not only helps co-workers to stop interrupting each other, but also helps individuals to focus.

Other suggestions from our users include "Gotta minute?" meetings and Office Hours. For "Gotta Minute?" meetings, colleagues arrange meet once a day to ask questions or get input from each other on issues rather than interrupting each other as each issues come up. The CAPTURE page is great for collecting these issues for "Gotta Minute?" meetings.

Office Hours work just like they do in college, except they are held by a supervisor. A supervisor of her department wanted to set some limits on the constant questions coming her way. She decided to set aside 15 minutes in both the morning and afternoon for employees to ask questions. Employees were directed to write down their questions and present them at this time.

Go ahead and venture into starting these conversations with your team members and create your own ways to help each other minimize unnecessary interruptions that can be avoided or postponed until one is finished with their focused session. And for those interruptions that can't be avoided, use the NOW method, including MicroPlanning™ to help you manage them well and strive even in a world of constant interruptions.

# Chapter 10

# End-of-Day

# Reconciliation

# How it Works

Simply put, this consists of reviewing your journal and identifying outstanding tasks and issues, and planning their completion. In the larger scheme of things, and according to the Accomplishing More in Less Time, With Less Effort, and Less Stress methodology[20], this would also involve reconciling your calendar and your e-mail and potentially other information stores or workspaces. In this discussion, we will cover the journal reconciliation and your e-mail, which typically involves the following:

**Reconciling the Today's page in your journal:** You review each item and decide if the item was completed and if additional action is needed. If the item was not completed, then you plan its completion. This may consist of completing it right now at reconciliation time if at all

---

20 *The Accomplishing More With Less Workbook* covers the full reconciliation process including beginning-of-day and end-of-day activities.

possible, or potentially reserving time on your calendar to complete it tomorrow or at a later date, or simply putting the appropriate reminder. Sometimes even if an item is complete, you may still have some follow-up action to plan for, such as a follow-up with a customer or a team member based on a discussion that took place today.

**Then reconciling the Capture page:** The process is similar to the one described for the Today's page above. You may also consider visiting the Capture page a few times during the day and work on or plan for some of these items as applicable.

Then reconciling the NOW pages: The NOW pages are likely to have some tasks that got interrupted and are still incomplete. The switch symbol is your best guide. Review the switch symbols to determine if any of these tasks are still outstanding and require follow-up. Review also the Next and your MicroPlans and look for any outstanding tasks or steps.

**Then reconciling e-mail:** This involved revisiting your "Today" e-mail category, and handling the messages that you said you wanted to handle today. Revisiting this category needs to happen several times during the day, potentially once in the mid morning, and again in the early afternoon and/or mid afternoon, and then for sure at the end of the day to handle any outstanding messages as part of the end of day reconciliation.

If there are important messages in the "Today" category that you can't possibly handle today, consider setting your stakeholders' expectations by replying to them briefly indicating you are aware of the issues at hand and giving them some indication of the timeframe for the next steps. If this involves tasks that are likely to take some time or have a deadline associated with them, the next step would be to schedule them on your calendar instead of just having them hidden in e-mail.

# Deeper Meaning

In a busy work environment with many competing priorities, it is difficult or impossible at times to deliver what was expected or what we promised. The end-of-day reconciliation presents an opportunity to update our stakeholders about critical deliverables that were in the works today, and reset their expectations if necessary.

Overall, the end-of-day reconciliation is mostly about closing the loops on open issues and tasks, instead of being surprised later by missed deadlines, broken promises, and issues falling through the cracks, all diminishing productivity, damaging working relationships, and increasing stress.

It is also an opportunity to reflect on the day, and thinking strategically about what happened, acknowledge our accomplishments, and ponder or journal on lessons learned. Without such reflections, days go by too quickly, accomplishments are ignored, and lessons are overlooked, all ingredients for a robotic life that keeps repeating itself, robbing us the opportunity to learn, get motivated, be creative, and feel accomplished.

The Perfect Day Method, and its structured use of the journal and timer, helps you become more aware of time and how you use your time. As you go through the day, the method keeps you focused and more purposeful--which also means strategic, and at the end of the day, not only would you have accomplished much more and felt far better, but you have plenty of data to show what you have accomplished, and to help you address what you haven't accomplished. With the Perfect Day Method, the days, at the end of which you feel exhausted because you worked non-stop and yet wonder what you have accomplished, are officially over. Welcome to the Perfect Day, which is a day to celebrate, learn from, and grow from!

# Discoveries

At the end of the day, the journal transitions from being a tool for focus to being an informative record of our time. While reconciling your journal, you may discover how you actually spend your time is not what you expected. Users sometimes notice how little time they actually have between interruptions - sometimes less than 15 minutes! Others may notice a discrepancy between priority tasks and the tasks they end up spending most of their time on. In one such case, Tiffany Conn was able to use her Perfect Day journal to negotiate a better use of her time.

*"The list was a real eye opener as to where my time goes every day. When you break it down and account for blocks of time like that in detail with tasks assigned it really makes clear what tasks are eating your time. Then you can utilize it to evaluate if those are really the most important tasks.*

I was able to determine what tasks are weighing me down. I identified a process today that we have all thought took a lot of time but I can now quantify how much time it takes which is important for evaluating the process. We are auditors and when faced with hard data we make changes.

By analyzing the time I spend on each activity in this much detail allowed me to provide the executives in my organization with the evidence needed to get some of the clerical duties I was doing switched to a technician so I could focus on the tasks that really add value to our organization. I didn't realize how much money they were paying me for data entry and neither did they until [using the Perfect Day Method.]

...I am very thankful that I finally noted all of the time spent on these activities and got this change made. I can already feel myself having more time to spend on the value added activities."

# Chapter 11

# Mindfulness @Work

# Mindfulness Now!

There is growing scientific evidence that mindfulness and mindfulness practices have concrete physical and mental health benefits ranging from lowering blood pressure, to reducing cortisol levels--the stress hormone associated with stress and anxiety, strengthening the immune system, improving sleep quality, emotional stability, ability to focus, ability to switch tasks and manage attention, among other things. Mindfulness practices are believed to change the structure of the brain in a positive way to create lasting changes. MRI scans showed that mindfulness practices reduced activity in the amygdala, the part of the brain mostly responsible for fear and anxiety, while increasing activity in the prefrontal cortex responsible for thinking, decision-making, and empathizing. Mindfulness is no longer only for yogis, but it is gaining popularity everywhere including organizations in health care, governmental institutions, and Silicon Valley companies. Google for instance installed a labyrinth for employees to practice walking meditation as part of the Search Inside Yourself mindfulness program founded by Chade-Meng Tan.

## Mindfulness simply defined

Mindfulness, simply put, is paying attention to what is happening around us and within us without reacting to it[21]. It is the ability to be in the present moment without distraction and without judgment. Mindfulness practices can move our brains toward being less stressed and more productive. Such practices cause one to pay attention to his or her present thoughts, body sensations, emotions, without passing judgment or reacting. Mindfulness is important because typically, so much of what is going on in our heads is compulsive thinking about the future or the past. We miss out on actual life because we're too busy planning for the next thing. We can make a difficult time much worse for ourselves if we

---

[21] Extracted from *Time for Leadership*, chapter 9, contributed by Alicia Ruelaz Maher, M.D.

continue to overthink it. The ultimate goal is to incorporate mindfulness into all areas of your life, to notice when you are out of the present moment, and to engage your senses to get back into it.

# PDM is mindfulness @work

PDM puts mindfulness in your workday and turns mindfulness into a habit; a way of working. Here is how:

First, the NOW tag prompts you to be decisive on which task you're about to take on now. This, in and of itself, engages your active thinking and brings you to the present moment. Instead of hastily making decisions based on temptation, anxiety, or acts of randomness, you make more informed decisions based on wisdom by taking into consideration current reality and desired results (mindful task selection). Once you decide on the NOW task and write it down, the timer keeps you aware of time and keeps your attention on the task throughout the 15-minute timeframe (mindful task execution).

Second, the MicroPlan™ helps you dissect the NOW task into smaller steps, deepening your understanding of the NOW task, engaging your active thinking even further, and providing you the framework you need to be able to recover when your mind wanders or you get otherwise interrupted (returning to the present moment).

Third, the NEXT column, CAPTURE page, and TODAY page, all help you notice and capture thoughts about things to do, allowing you to jot down these items quickly and easily, and return to the NOW task (again returning to the present moment).

Fourth, PDM encourages you to notice thoughts and emotions, and use the THOUGHT and EMOTION tags to label them, rank them, and move beyond them, or decide to work through them now or later. As described earlier in the book, in the Thoughts and Emotions Chapter, labeling and ranking is proven to engage the higher order parts of the brain associated with thinking and planning instead of experiencing reactivity (mindfulness instead of reactivity). In this process we learn to let go of the thought or feeling bothering us. This is one of the foundational principles of mindfulness. According to Chade-Meng Tan, holding on - whether by refusing to let something go or by refusing to let something come - is what Buddhist meditators identify as the main cause of human suffering.

Instead, now that you have experienced your emotion as a bodily sensation and identified it, recognize that your thoughts and emotions are simply things you feel – they do not define you.

And there is more. Keep on reading!

# The 15-minute mark as your mindfulness stop

How about taking the 15-minute mark a step further? When your timer is up, this is the "perfect" reminder to take a moment to bring yourself to the present moment and pay attention to your thoughts, body sensations, emotions, without passing judgment, just noticing. Use the THOUGHT and EMOTION tags if you notice thoughts and feelings that need to be recognized and put to rest, especially related to worries about the past or the future.

The 15-minute mark is also a good time to engage in a brief breathing exercise, a way to get mindful while delivering more oxygen to the body and the brain, and calming yourself down. I don't have time, you might say. How about nine seconds? Internally count to three with deep inhalation, then hold your breath for three, and then exhale for three. If you have a minute, repeat this six times, and resume your next task or activity with more oxygen and a more open mind.

# 15 minutes of mindfulness meditation

How about taking this even further and dedicating a whole 15 minutes for mindfulness meditation? If this sounds way out of reach, place this idea on the back burner for now and revisit it if/when the time is right. If this sounds intriguing, even just a bit intriguing, it is probably time for you to explore this topic further.

The most basic form of mindfulness meditation, as described by some of the thought leaders in this field such as Jon Kabat-Zinn[22], includes sitting in a comfortable position, with eyes closed, and focusing on your breath and the rhythm and sensation of breathing. When you notice your mind wandering and you're no longer focused on the breath, you acknowledge this without reprimanding yourself and without going further into the

---

[22] Jon Kabat-Zinn author of Wherever Your Go, There You Are, and Full Catastrophe Living, among others.

interrupting thoughts.  You simply go back to the breathing and focus on the sensation of the breath.

An even simpler type of meditation as described as the "Easier Way" by Chade-Meng Tan, is to simply sit without an agenda.[23] You can of course, alternate between the two kinds of meditation. In fact, this is encouraged because it allows you to practice two different kinds of attention. Focusing on the breath requires focused attention and simply sitting and being is a practice requires open attention.

Over time, you will feel calmer, less absorbed by past and future thoughts, and better able to focus and better manage your attention! All these things are crucial in today's work environment and in life. Researchers from the University of Washington for instance, in a study from 2012, tested participants' ability to perform multiple tasks in a work

---

[23] Tan, Chade-Meng. *Search inside Yourself: The Unexpected Path to Achieving Success, Happiness (and World Peace)*. New York: HarperOne, 2012.

setting. They found that mindfulness practices over an eight-week period, improved the participants' ability to switch between tasks and to monitor their attention resulting in a more effective overall management of attention and related mental resources.

A new tag is born:

NOW: Mindfulness Meditation (15)

# PDM and Mindfulness @work, the road to accomplishment and happiness

Here are ways in which PDM and mindfulness at work translate to significant accomplishments and a happier you:

**First: Accomplishments require paying attention and this is exactly what PDM enables us to do.** It is only by paying attention that we are able to be most effective and accomplish meaningful things. When paying attention to what is going on now, we make better decisions, take more effective actions, and are likely to have bigger and more positive impact on the present and the future. PDM helps us manage our attention and keep it on the NOW task and therefore be most effective now and in the future.

**Second: Accomplishments require getting deeper into our tasks and this is exactly what PDM enables us to do**. Getting deeper enables us to a) think strategically and creatively, b) address the root causes instead of simply putting out quick fixes over and over again, and c) envision and implement innovative solutions to the problems at hand. The NEXT column, CAPTURE page, and TODAY page, together with the THOUGHT and EMOTION tags, all keep us focused and allow us to get deeper. At the end of each 15-minute timeframe, if needed, we can renew for another 15 minutes and get even deeper.

**Third: Stress is one of the prevalent workplace challenges and this is exactly what PDM enables us to reduce.** When we are in the NOW task, and have our MicroPlan™ and other PDM tools and techniques handy, we are truly thinking about the NOW task. We are no longer thinking about worries from the past or concerns about the future. Our work on the NOW task is engaging our prefrontal cortex and making us less prone to fear and anxiety. This is stress reduction at its best.

**Fourth: Happiness is not a destination but the enjoyment of the journey and this is exactly what PDM enables us to experience**. It is more common in a typical workday to go from one task to the next, immediately getting consumed by the next task, and then the next one, robbing ourselves the opportunity to enjoy what we have accomplished. PDM built-in small time increments and tags help us rediscover the joy of making progress, and the pleasures of the journey, as opposed to being overly fixated on the end goal.

In essence, PDM injects mindfulness into our workday and helps us transform from a robotic worker, to a fully strategic and creative player, appreciating and enjoying current reality, while creating a significantly better future.

# Appendix: More Offerings from People-OnTheGo

# Where to go from here?

Here are some resources to help you further with PDM and beyond:

- The Perfect 15-Minute Day Journal
- The Perfect 15-Minute Day online course on-demand
- *The Accomplishing More With Less Workbook* and related Workshop and Webinars
- The *Time for Leadership* Book
- The Accomplishing More With Less for Managers Workshop and Webinars
- The Accomplishing More With Less Leadership Program
- The Design Thinking to Focus, Collaborate, and Play Workshop
- In addition to a variety of technology and productivity webinars

Visit www.theperfect15minuteday.com and www.people-onthego.com for more details.

# Works Cited

Ballard, Dawna. "Finding Balance in an Age of Always-On Business: The Time-Space Mixtape." Presentation at Collabosphere, Austin, TX, September 27-30, 2015.

Ballard, Dawna, and Sunshine Webster. "Time and Time Again: The Search for Meaning/fulness Through Popular Discourse on the Time and Timing of Work."*KronoScope* 8, no. 2 (2009): 131-45.

Dweck, Carol S. *Mindset: The New Psychology of Success*. New York: Random House, 2006.

González, Victor M., and Gloria Mark. ""Constant, Constant, Multi-tasking Craziness"" *Proceedings of the 2004 Conference on Human Factors in Computing Systems - CHI '04*, 2004.

Greist-Bousquet, S., Schiffman, N. (1992). The effect of Task interruption and closure on perceived duration. Bulletin of the Psychonomic Society, 30(1), 9-11.

Harris, Dan. *10% Happier: How I Tamed the Voice in My Head, Reduced Stress without Losing My Edge, and Found Self-help That Actually Works: A True Story.*

Lazar, S. W., Kerr, C. E., Wasserman, R. H., Gray, J. R., Greve, D. N., Treadway, M. T., ... Fischl, B. (2005). "Meditation Experience Is Associated with Increased Cortical Thickness."*NeuroReport* 16, no. 17 (2005): 1893-897.

Mark, Gloria, Daniela Gudith, and Ulrich Klocke. "The Cost of Interrupted Work."*Proceeding of the Twenty-sixth Annual CHI Conference on Human Factors in Computing Systems - CHI '08*, 2008.

Mark, Gloria, Victor M. Gonzalez, and Justin Harris. "No Task Left Behind?"*Proceedings of the SIGCHI Conference on Human Factors in Computing Systems - CHI '05*, 2005.

Richard Davidson, et al., "Alterations in Brain and Immune Function Produced by Mindfulness Meditation," *Psychosomatic Medicine* 65, no. 4 (2003): 564-570

Ruelaz Maher, Alicia. *From Scattered to Centered: Understanding and Transforming the Distracted Brain*. CreateSpace Independent Publishing Platform, 2013.

Stephens, Keri K., Jaehee K. Cho, and Dawna I. Ballard. "Simultaneity, Sequentiality, and Speed: Organizational Messages About Multiple-Task Completion." *Human Communication Research* 38, no. 1 (2012): 23-47.

Tan, Chade-Meng. *Search inside Yourself: The Unexpected Path to Achieving Success, Happiness (and World Peace)*. New York: HarperOne, 2012.

Made in the USA
San Bernardino, CA
10 June 2016